DATE DUE			
FEB 3			

Discard

972
CAS

Casagrande, Louis B.

Focus on Mexico.

111176

GOLDEN SIERRA HIGH SCHOOL

FOCUS ON MEXICO

FOCUS ON
MEXICO

Modern Life in an Ancient Land

Louis B. Casagrande

Sylvia A. Johnson

Photographs by Phillips Bourns

Lerner Publications Company
Minneapolis

ACKNOWLEDGMENTS The photographs in this book have been provided by Phillips Bourns with the exception of the following: pp. 11, 17, Mexican National Tourist Council; pp. 12, 13, 19 (bottom), 32, National Archives; p. 14, S. A. Johnson; p. 19 (top), National Air and Space Museum; pp. 22, 27, Sumner W. Matteson, courtesy of the Science Museum of Minnesota; pp. 29, 30, 31, Bazar de Fotografia Casasola; pp. 34, 71, 88, Louis B. Casagrande; p. 40, Wide World Photos, Inc.; p. 53, Bell Helicopter Textron Company; pp. 85, 86, Christiana Dittmann

Library of Congress Cataloging-in-Publication Data

Casagrande, Louis B.
  Focus on Mexico

  Includes index.
  Summary: Examines the diversity of life in modern Mexico, its peoples and complex cultural heritage, and how past and present combine in a blend of cultures.
    1. Mexico—Civilization—Juvenile literature.
2. Youth—Mexico—Juvenile literature. [1. Mexico—Civilization]
I. Johnson, Sylvia A. II. Bourns, Phillips, ill. III. Title.
F1210.C385 1986   972   85-23829
ISBN 0-8225-0645-9 (lib. bdg.)
    2   3   4   5   6   7   8   9   10   95   94   93   92   91   90   89   88   87

CONTENTS

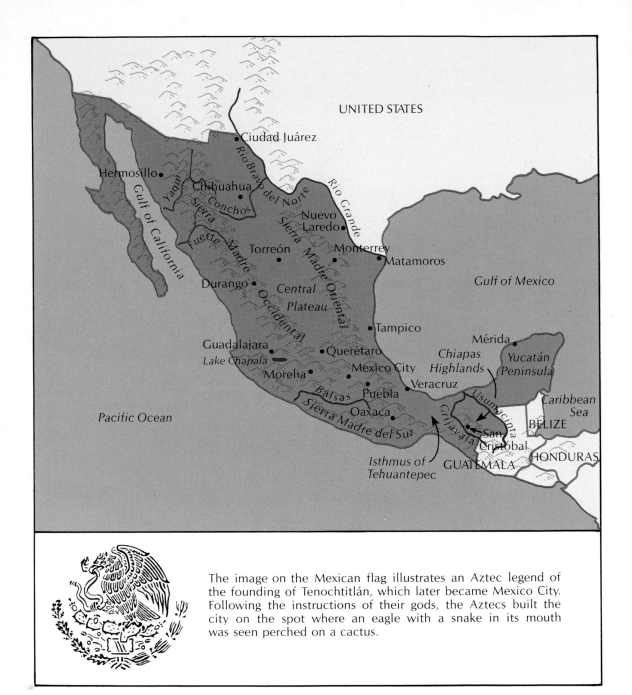

UNITED STATES

Ciudad Juárez

Hermosillo

Gulf of California

Yaqui

Chihuahua

Conchos

Rio Bravo del Norte

Rio Grande

Nuevo Laredo

Sierra Madre Occidental

Sierra Madre Oriental

Fuerte

Torreón

Monterrey

Matamoros

Durango

Central Plateau

Gulf of Mexico

Tampico

Guadalajara

Lake Chapala

Querétaro

Mexico City

Mérida

Chiapas Highlands

Yucatán Peninsula

Morelia

Puebla

Veracruz

Usumacinta

Caribbean Sea

Balsas

Oaxaca

Sierra Madre del Sur

Grijalva

BELIZE

Pacific Ocean

San Cristóbal

HONDURAS

Isthmus of Tehuantepec

GUATEMALA

The image on the Mexican flag illustrates an Aztec legend of the founding of Tenochtitlán, which later became Mexico City. Following the instructions of their gods, the Aztecs built the city on the spot where an eagle with a snake in its mouth was seen perched on a cactus.

6

INTRODUCTION

Everywhere in Mexico, the past is preserved in great monuments of stone. Just north of Mexico City are the massive pyramids of the Sun and Moon, built more than 2,000 years ago without the use of the wheel or metal tools. Along the coastline of the Yucatán Peninsula, the towers and temples of ruined Mayan cities look out over the blue-green waters of the Caribbean Sea. On the Central Plateau, in Mexico's heartland, 400-year-old Spanish churches hold a place of honor on the plazas of quiet colonial towns.

Although monuments from the past are everywhere in Mexico, signs of the present are evident too. Along foot trails once used by the merchants of the Aztec empire, huge diesel trucks carry the hardware of an industrial society. From mountain peaks that were once shrines to ancient gods, microwave relay stations transmit television signals to remote mountain villages. In the Valley of Mexico, the site of the splendid Aztec capital, Tenochtitlán, 18 million people now live crowded together in a great modern metropolis.

Today the ancient land of Mexico is the home of a modern developing nation, where there are as many factory smokestacks on the horizon as there are ruined temples and cities. In the past 20 years, Mexican society has been transformed by economic change, with industries booming and cities growing rapidly. Yet the ancient monuments still stand and the past lives on in the values and beliefs of the Mexican people.

Despite its ancient heritage, Mexico is one of the youngest countries in the world, with more than half of its population under the age of 17. These young Mexicans—nearly 50 million of them—have felt the impact of the changes that have taken place in the nation's life. Today they are confronted with new opportunities and new choices in a world that includes both factories and ancient pyramids, giant modern cities and remote mountain villages.

To get a clear picture of modern Mexico, it is important to understand both its past and its present—to look closely at the nation's complex history and at the lives, hopes, and dreams of young Mexicans today.

8

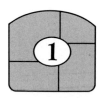

A HISTORY OF THREE CULTURES

Located not far from the Zócalo, the main plaza of Mexico City, is a square known as La Plaza de las Tres Culturas, the Plaza of the Three Cultures. It was given this name because the structures located on the square symbolize the three "cultures" or traditions whose histories have created the complex Mexico of today.

The first and earliest of the cultures—Mexico's Indian heritage—is represented by the ruins of an Aztec temple that stand in the middle of the plaza. Nearby is a building that symbolizes the culture of the Spanish conquerors who destroyed the Aztec civilization. It is the church and convent of Santiago de Tlatelolco, built by Spanish friars in 1609.

The other structures on the plaza are sleek glass-and-concrete office buildings that form a sharp contrast to the restored ruins and the thick-walled church. These buildings, one of which houses Mexico's Ministry of Foreign Relations, represent the modern culture that has brought such changes to Mexican life in recent years.

Better than any other monument or historic site, the Plaza of the Three Cultures dramatizes the way in which the Indian, the Spanish, and the modern exist side by side in Mexico today, not only in architecture but also in the lives of the Mexican people.

The Indian Legacy

The temple that stands in the Plaza of the Three Cultures is Aztec, and it is this Indian group that is most glorified in the museums and myths of modern Mexico. The Aztecs, however, built their empire on the contributions of many earlier Indian civilizations.

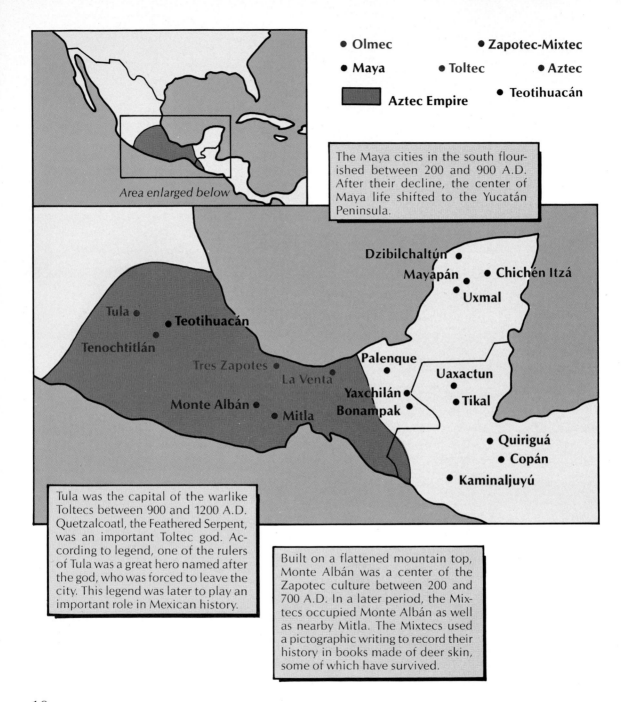

● Olmec ● Zapotec-Mixtec
● Maya ● Toltec ● Aztec
■ Aztec Empire ● Teotihuacán

The Maya cities in the south flourished between 200 and 900 A.D. After their decline, the center of Maya life shifted to the Yucatán Peninsula.

Area enlarged below

Dzibilchaltún
Mayapán ● Chichén Itzá
Uxmal

Tula ●
● Teotihuacán
Tenochtitlán

Tres Zapotes ● Palenque
La Venta Uaxactun
Yaxchilán ●
Monte Albán ● Bonampak ● Tikal
● Mitla

● Quiriguá
● Copán
● Kaminaljuyú

Tula was the capital of the warlike Toltecs between 900 and 1200 A.D. Quetzalcoatl, the Feathered Serpent, was an important Toltec god. According to legend, one of the rulers of Tula was a great hero named after the god, who was forced to leave the city. This legend was later to play an important role in Mexican history.

Built on a flattened mountain top, Monte Albán was a center of the Zapotec culture between 200 and 700 A.D. In a later period, the Mixtecs occupied Monte Albán as well as nearby Mitla. The Mixtecs used a pictographic writing to record their history in books made of deer skin, some of which have survived.

Some of the most impressive artistic creations of the Olmecs were enormous stone heads like the one shown here. Weighing as much as 40 tons and standing 8 to 9 feet high, these massive heads may be portraits of Olmec rulers.

THE OLMEC

One of the earliest civilizations in Mesoamerica was that of the Olmecs, whose cities on the Gulf Coast dominated the area from about 1200 B.C. to 250 A.D.
Like the Greeks of the Old World, the Olmecs had a genius for science and philosophy as well as art. They were the first astronomers of ancient America, and they used their observations of the sun and the stars to create a precise calendar.
In religion, the Olmecs developed a concept of the universe that influenced all the succeeding peoples of the region. Their chief deity, a powerful god who took the form of a jaguar, was worshipped by many other Mesoamerican cultures.

The city of Palenque, located in the modern Mexican state of Chiapas, was an important center of Maya life between 600 and 700 A.D. This drawing of the ruined city was made by an English artist, Frederick Catherwood, in the 1850s.

THE MAYA

Another of the great early civilizations of Mesoamerica was created by the Maya between the years 300 B.C. and 900 A.D. These ancient people adopted and improved the Olmec calendar and invented a system of hieroglyphic writing that they used to record the histories of their rulers on impressive stone monuments. Maya cities like Palenque, Tikal, and Yaxchilán, located in dense rain forest, were built around magnificent stone temples that stood on top of steep pyramids. Between 700 and 900 A.D., many of these large cities were destroyed or abandoned by their inhabitants. Many aspects of Maya culture lived on, however, in the art and traditions of the modern Maya.

These drawings by Catherwood are based on some of the elegant sculptures found at Palenque. Today, archaeologists are able to identify many of the people portrayed in the sculptures and to describe their lives and histories.

Thanks to modern advances in interpreting the Mayas' hieroglyphic writing, we now know that the scene below shows Lord Pacal (right), an important ruler of Palenque, with his mother, Lady Zac-Kuk. The symbols above and to the right of the two figures include hieroglyphs of their names.

Lord Pacal ruled Palenque from 615 A.D. until his death in 683. He was buried in a magnificent tomb, which has been found beneath a temple-pyramid in the city. Pacal was succeeded by his son Chan-Bahlum, who is shown dressed in kingly splendor in the drawing on the left. The glyphs in this scene describe the transfer of power between the two great Maya rulers.

13

TEOTIHUACAN

At the same time that the Maya cities thrived in the southern part of Mesoamerica, the powerful civilization of Teotihuacán controlled the central area of the region. The city of Teotihuacán, located in the Valley of Mexico north of present-day Mexico City, was first settled around 300 B.C. By 500 A.D., it had a population that has been estimated at 200,000, larger than most European cities in the same period. Like other ancient cities of Mesoamerica, Teotihuacán was built around a ceremonial center made up of great temple-pyramids. (The massive Pyramid of the Moon is shown on the opposite page.) The outlying areas of the city included houses, workshops, and apartment complexes that today cover more than 12 square miles of territory.

Teotihuacán fell to invaders around 650 A.D., but the influence of the city on the civilizations of Mesoamerica lasted for many centuries. When the Aztecs came to the Valley of Mexico, they looked with awe at the ruins of the great metropolis and gave it the name Teotihuacán—the Place of the Gods.

One of the chief gods of Teotihuacán was Quetzalcoatl, the Feathered Serpent, shown here in a carving from a temple dedicated to his worship. Also honored by the Olmecs and the Maya, Quetzalcoatl was a god of culture and learning, very different from the warlike deities of later Indian civilizations.

Over 150 feet tall, the Pyramid of the Moon towers over a complex of buildings at one end of Teotihuacán's broad main avenue. The structure's brick-and-rubble surface was once covered by smooth slabs of stone.

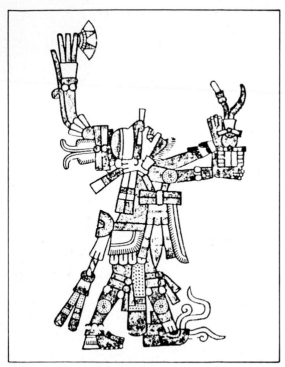

According to legend, the war god Huitzilopochtli led the Aztecs from their northern homeland to settle in the Valley of Mexico. This drawing of the fierce god comes from one of the few surviving Aztec books.

The tribe known as the Aztecs or Mexicas first appeared in the Valley of Mexico around 1200 A.D., many years after leaving Aztlan, their mysterious homeland in the north. Untutored in the arts and sciences of the earlier Indian civilizations, the Aztecs were warriors who gradually conquered the settled people in the valley. In the process, they took many captives to be sacrificed to their bloodthirsty war gods.

By the early 1400s, the Aztecs had built two large cities on islands in shallow Lake Texcoco, which covered much of the area where Mexico City now stands. One city was Tlatelolco, a busy commercial center located on the site of the modern Plaza of the Three Cultures. This community was connected by causeway to the Aztec capital, Tenochtitlán, whose great main square occupied the area now comprising the Zócalo in Mexico City. On the square were erected enormous temples and elaborate palaces where Aztec kings such as Moctezuma I and Moctezuma II lived in splendor, absolute rulers of an empire with more inhabitants than many countries in Europe.

By the time that the Spanish reached Mexico in 1519, the population of Tenochtitlán and its surrounding communities had reached 300,000. Food to feed the city was grown on hundreds of *chinampas*, gardens formed by mud-covered rafts that floated in the waters of Lake Texcoco. The abundant products of the *chinampas* were displayed in the great market at Tlatelolco, along with amber, jade, feathers, fine textiles, and cacao beans brought from distant regions. These exotic goods were imported by the *pochteca*, Aztec merchants who journeyed throughout Mesoamerica along the old Olmec/Teotihuacán trade routes.

A mural by the modern Mexican artist Diego Rivera showing the Aztec market at Tlatelolco. In the upper right corner of the painting can be seen the central square of Tenochtitlán with its tall pyramids. Bernal Díaz, one of Hernan Cortes' soldiers, was amazed at his first sight of the bustling market. He wrote later in his account of the Spanish Conquest, "We beheld on the lake a great multitude of canoes, some coming with supplies of food, others returning loaded with cargoes of merchandise.... Our soldiers, who had been in Constantinople, in Rome and all over Italy, said they had never seen a market so well laid out, so orderly and so full of people."

17

No longer barbarians, the Aztecs had adopted many of the traditions and beliefs of their predecessors. They worshipped Quetzalcoatl and the jaguar god as well as their own fierce god of war, Huitzilopochtli. Like the Indian civilizations before them, the Aztecs studied the movements of the sun, moon, and stars to know when to plant corn and when to offer sacrifices to the powers that ruled their world.

With the coming of the Spanish, much of Mexico's Indian civilization was destroyed. Acting in the name of a Catholic God and the Spanish Crown, the *conquistador* Hernán Cortés invaded the country in February 1519. He marched toward Tenochtitlán with his 600 men, horses, cannons, and attack dogs, making alliances along the way with the many enemies of the Aztecs. With their aid, Cortés succeeded in defeating the greatest empire of pre-Hispanic America.

THE RETURN OF QUETZALCOATL

Aztec legends played a strange and fateful role in the Spanish conquest of the Indian civilization. The Aztecs were familiar with stories about a great ruler of ancient times, named after the god Quetzalcoatl, who had been exiled but had promised to return to his people. The year predicted for his return was Ce Acatl (One Reed), one of the 52 years in the recurring cycle of the Aztec calendar. Hernán Cortés and his army landed on the shores of Mexico in February 1519, which was Ce Acatl in the Aztec calendar. The emperor Moctezuma II soon received reports about these strangers in his land, led by a man fair-skinned and bearded even as Quetzalcoatl had been. Moctezuma suspected that the legendary hero was returning to claim his throne, as prophesied. His suspicion was reinforced by the occurrence of many strange and frightening omens, including the appearance of a bright comet during the daylight hours.

When Cortés began his march toward Tenochtitlán, Moctezuma sent ambassadors bearing gifts to meet him. Although he commanded a large army, the emperor did not resist the advance of the small group of Spaniards, fearing that their leader was Quetzalcoatl himself. By the time the Aztecs realized that Cortés was not the returning god/hero but an ambitious and ruthless man, resistance was too late.

Moctezuma observes the omen of the comet from the roof of his palace. This drawing is from a book about the Aztecs written after the Conquest by a Spanish friar, Diego Durán, and illustrated by Indian artists.

An illustration from a history of New Spain written by another priest, Bernardino de Sahagún, showing the meeting between Cortés and Moctezuma's ambassadors.

During and after the Conquest, nearly 6 million Indians—two-thirds of the native population—were killed or died from European diseases. The conquerors also burned hundreds of books and persecuted Indian priests, effectively destroying 3,000 years of learning in architecture, mathematics, and astronomy. Today archaeologists find only the physical evidence of these great intellectual achievements.

Not all aspects of Indian culture were destroyed, however, and some survive even today. The contemporary Mexican diet consists of many foods known to the Aztecs, including 100 varieties of corn, dozens of kinds of beans, squash, chiles, tomatoes, avocados, and chocolate. Náhuatl, the Aztec language, is still spoken in Mexico, and many Náhuatl words have become part of Mexican Spanish. (Some Náhuatl words have even found their way into the English language.)

The form of Roman Catholicism practiced in Mexico has also been influenced by the country's Indian past. Catholic saints are often identified with the old local gods and goddesses, and many fiestas in Indian villages feature dances and costumes that would have been familiar to the Maya and Aztecs. Even in the folk art and fine art of modern Mexico, images of the jaguar and the feathered serpent are prominent, recalling the ancient beliefs of the Indian people of Mesoamerica.

19

From New Spain to a New Nation

After the fall of the Aztec capital in 1521, the Spanish *conquistadores* marched west and south to seek their fortunes and to tame the remaining Indian tribes of Mexico. At first, the defeated Indians were treated as slaves and were forced to pay tribute to their conquerors in return for protection. Soon, however, the Spanish king began to take control of the territory won by Cortés, now known as the colony of New Spain. The conqueror and his daring followers were gradually replaced by government officials sent from Spain to administer the king's laws and by Catholic priests bringing the blessings of salvation to a pagan land.

While Franciscan and Dominican missionaries devoted themselves to the spiritual welfare of the Indians, other Spaniards were more interested in Indian labor. Many Indian workers were needed on the *haciendas*, large tracts of land that were granted to Spanish landowners by the king during the late 1500s and early 1600s. Indians were employed to cultivate the fields, tend animals, and cut firewood while living in miserable huts erected around the walls of the *casa grande*, the "big house" of the wealthy landowner. Because their wages were so low, the workers were forced to borrow from the *hacienda* store for any emergency. Through these loans, the landowners were able to control the lives of the Indians employed on their estates.

Indians made up the lowest social and economic level of the complicated society that developed in New Spain during the colonial era. At the top of the social ladder were the *peninsulares*, Spaniards from Spain who came to the colony usually as administrators or religious officials. Inferior to the *peninsulares* in position and power were the *criollos*, those of Spanish blood who were born in Mexico. Both groups of Spaniards were considered superior to the *mestizos*, people of mixed Spanish and Indian heritage usually born of unions between Spanish men and Indian women.

The church of Sacro Monte in the town of Amecameca was built by Spanish missionaries during the 1500s. Like many colonial churches, it was constructed on the site of an Aztec temple.

The courtyard of a *hacienda* near Mexico City where both humans and animals have been locked up for the night. This photograph was taken in the early 20th century, but it illustrates conditions that had existed in Mexico since colonial times.

As the years passed, the *mestizos* became the largest racial group in the colony. Despite their numbers, however, most of these people of mixed blood occupied a position almost as low as that of the Indians at the bottom of Mexican society.

By the early 1800s, New Spain was torn by internal conflict between the two groups of Spaniards in the colony. The *criollos* fiercely resented their inferior position and the rule imposed by the *peninsulares*, who were frequently called by the nickname *gachupines*. (The name came from a Náhuatl word meaning "men with spurs.") Inspired by the successes of the American and French revolutions, the Mexican-born Spaniards saw the possibility of freedom from Spain and the formation of an independent nation.

On September 16, 1810, Miguel Hidalgo y Costilla, a *criollo* parish priest in the village of Dolores, began the Mexican War of Independence with an impassioned speech in which he cried out, "Mexicans, long live Mexico! Death to the Gachupines!" Hidalgo's Grito de Dolores (Cry of Dolores) set off a struggle that lasted 11 long years. The conflict brought death to some 600,000 Mexicans, including Hidalgo himself, Ignacio Allende, José María Morelos, and many others who are now remembered as the heroes of Mexico's liberation.

The independent nation of Mexico was finally established in 1821, but the loss of so many lives and the economic chaos of the war had created problems that could not be easily solved. More confusion was caused by a political struggle between those who wanted the new nation to be a republic, with an elected president and congress, and others who wanted the country to be ruled by a king. In 1824, the warring groups finally agreed on a constitution that made Mexico a republic with a federal form of government similiar to that of the United States.

During this early period of nationhood, Mexico not only suffered internal conflict but also experienced serious problems on the northern border that she shared with the United States. In 1821, the northern Mexican province of Texas had been settled by 300 American families, led by Stephen Austin. Ten years later, the non-Mexican population of the province outnumbered the native Mexicans, and talk of independence from Mexico filled the air.

When the Texans declared their independence from the Mexican government in 1835, President Antonio López de Santa Anna led an army of 6,000 soldiers to put down the revolt. Santa Anna defeated the Texans at the Alamo in San Antonio, but a later battle led to the capture of the Mexican leader and his granting of Texan independence in 1836. Santa Anna's treaty with the Texans was not recognized by the Mexican government, however, and Mexicans still considered the "independent republic" of Texas a part of Mexico.

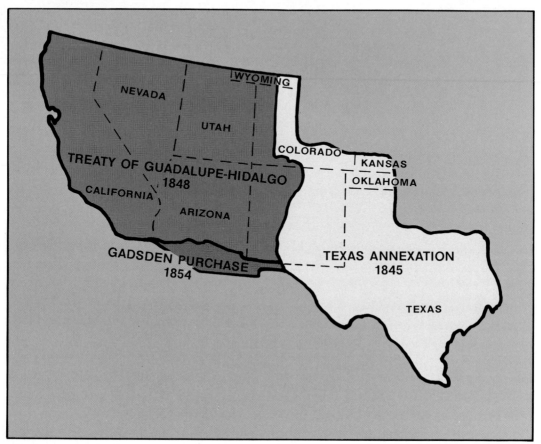

By the terms of the Treaty of Guadalupe-Hidalgo, Mexico was forced to cede or sell to the United States fully one-third of its territory. A later purchase transferred even more Mexican land to the United States. Because of these gains, the Giant of the North became a much larger country than its southern neighbor.

Almost 10 years after its revolt from Mexico, Texas was admitted to the American Union, and war broke out between the United States and Mexico over the disputed territory. The conflict lasted two years and ended only after American troops led by General Winfield Scott captured Mexico City on September 14, 1847. The next year, a defeated Mexican government was forced not only to recognize the loss of Texas but also to sell to the United States another enormous chunk of territory for the meager sum of $15 million.

This monument in Mexico City commemorates an important battle during the war between Mexico and the United States. When General Winfield Scott invaded the capital in September 1847, he met fierce resistance at Chapultepec Castle, which was defended by Mexican soldiers and young cadets from the Military Academy. American troops stormed the hill on which the castle stood, and the cadets fought to the end, some of them leaping from the walls rather than surrendering. Today the monument to the Niños Heroes—the Boy Heroes—stands at the foot of the famous hill, reminding Mexicans of a proud but tragic moment in their history.

Weakened by the war with the United States and humiliated by its loss of territory, Mexico found itself once more in a state of internal conflict and division. Among the factions that argued over the direction that the nation would take in the future was a group of liberal politicians and intellectuals opposed to Santa Anna and the other conservatives who had controlled the Mexican government since the early 1830s. This group was led by Benito Juárez, a full-blooded Zapotec Indian from Oaxaca. Juárez and his followers wanted to make liberal reforms that would allow freedom of work, trade, and education in Mexico as well as a reduction in the great power of the Roman Catholic Church.

In 1855, Juárez and the liberals took control of the government and began to implement some of their reforms. Their efforts were opposed by Mexico's conservative landowners and church leaders, who eventually sought outside help in defeating the liberals. The conservative faction encouraged the French emperor, Napoleon III, to invade Mexico, overthrow Juárez, and set up a traditional monarchy in place of the republic. In 1862, French troops occupied the country, and two years later, Napoleon III named Ferdinand Maximilian, Archduke of Austria, as emperor of Mexico.

For three years, Maximilian and his wife, Carlotta, ruled the nation from Chapultepec Castle, their elegant palace in Mexico City. The United States looked with disfavor on Maximilian's rule, disturbed by the fact that a neighboring country was under the control of a European power. Involved in its own Civil War, however, the American government could do nothing until 1865, when it put pressure on France to withdraw its forces. The French army left Mexico in 1867, and Juárez took over the government after defeating Maximilan and his supporters.

The liberal victory over the conservative forces did not last long. In 1877, the government was seized by an army general, Porfirio Díaz, who was to rule Mexico with an iron hand for the next 34 years. Instead of improving the living conditions of Mexico's poor, Díaz built railroads, increased the country's foreign trade, and made other changes that enriched the growing urban middle class. Supported by the army and the *rurales*, the dreaded rural police, Díaz brought order and growth to Mexico at the price of equality and freedom.

Members of the *rurales* on parade during the Cinco de Mayo (5th of May) celebration, 1907. The dictator Porfirio Díaz used this ruthless police force to maintain control in Mexico's rural areas.

Revolution and Modernization

One hundred years after the war for Mexican independence, the nation of Mexico was at war with itself. In 1910, the dictatorship of Porfirio Díaz, which had lasted for more than 30 years, fell apart as leaders calling for freedom and equality received increasing support from landless farmers and exploited workers.

A new Mexican revolution was underway.

One of the loudest voices in the Revolution of 1910 was that of Francisco Madero, a liberal leader of small stature and high ideals who argued for free elections and the rule of law. In his efforts to defeat Díaz and the conservative generals, Madero was joined by two very different men, Emiliano Zapata and Francisco "Pancho" Villa.

27

Zapata, an Indian from the state of Morelos in central Mexico, was the magnetic leader of an army of peasant farmers who were willing to fight to regain lands that had once been theirs. In the north, the revolutionary struggle was led by the bandit chieftain Pancho Villa. Villa and his cowboy army made devastating guerilla attacks against the great *haciendas* of powerful families like the Terrazas, who owned almost 6 billion acres of land in the state of Chihuahua.

In 1911, with rebellion breaking out all over Mexico, Díaz was forced to resign, and Francisco Madero took over the presidency. The revolution had seemingly come to a quick conclusion, but in fact, the struggle had just begun. In 1913, the followers of the deposed dictator Díaz, with the advice and assistance of United States ambassador Henry Lane Wilson, regained control of the government. Madero was assassinated, and rewards were offered for the heads of the rebel leaders Zapata and Villa.

Between 1913 and 1920, chaos reigned in Mexico as rival factions fought for control of the country. In 1914, Zapata and Villa, at the head of an army of 50,000 peasant soldiers, marched triumphantly into Mexico City. A few months later, however, they were defeated by another revolutionary leader, Venustiano Carranza, who was backed by two powerful generals, Alvaro Obregón and Plutarco Calles.

During the six years of Carranza's rule, a new constitution was drafted that embodied many of the social principles of the Revolution. (The Constitution of 1917 is still in force today.) But Emiliano Zapata and others believed that more extreme reforms were needed. Uprisings and bloodshed continued until 1919, when Zapata was killed.

The constant fighting of the revolutionary period took a tremendous toll on Mexico. Millions of Mexican citizens lost their lives. Tens of thousands fled the violence of their homeland, settling in Texas or California. The economy had been left in shambles, and in every city and town, there were homeless and starving people. This long and bitter chapter in Mexican history has inspired many novels and songs that commemorate the tragic events of the Revolution and celebrate its great heroes.

This historic photograph by Augustín Victor Casasola shows the first meeting of revolutionary leaders Pancho Villa (left, in ornate chair) and Emiliano Zapata (right), near Mexico City in 1914.

A powerful novel about the Revolution was *Los de Abajos* (usually translated as *The Underdogs*), written by Mariano Azuela and first published in 1915. This passage from the novel describes one of the greatest of the revolutionary heroes and legends:

'Villa's coming!' The news spread with the speed of lightning. Ah, Villa, the magic word. The great man, the idol; the invincible warrior who even from a distance exercises the fascination of a boa constrictor. . . . Ah, Villa! The battles of Juárez, Tierra Blanca, Chihuahua, Torreon! . . . Villa was the indomitable master of the sierra, the eternal victim of all governments who pursued him as though he were a wild beast. Villa was the reincarnation of the old legend: the bandit-benefactor who goes through the world with the lighted torch of an ideal: rob the rich to enrich the poor!

All Mexicans were touched by the violence of the Revolution, but women were particularly affected. Many lost their husbands, sons, fathers, their homes and livelihoods. Some women joined the revolutionary forces, serving as spies or smugglers of arms. Others became *soldaderas* and followed their men from battle to battle, acting as cooks, nurses, and, in some cases, soldiers themselves. These Casasola photographs show two brave women of the revolutionary period.

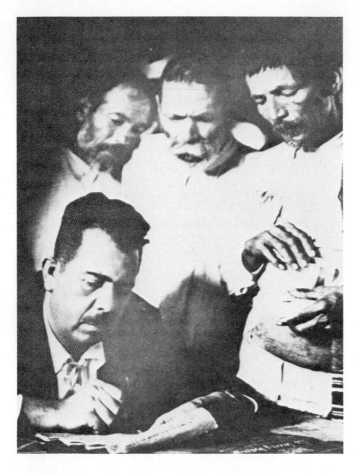

President Lázaro Cárdenas signs a land deed over to a group of peasant farmers.

The rebuilding of Mexico after the Revolution took nearly 20 years. True democracy, one of the main goals of the revolutionary leaders, was not achieved until Lázaro Cárdenas, governor of the state of Michoacán, became president in 1934.

During his six-year term, Cárdenas began the first serious land distribution program, creating *ejidos*, or communal farms, in hundreds of communities. He also nationalized the railroads and the oil industry, angering the U.S. and British companies that had dominated the Mexican economy since the days of Porfirio Díaz. These reforms made Cárdenas the favorite of the Mexican masses. His political party, today known as the Partido Revolucionario Institucional (PRI), has controlled Mexican politics ever since.

The next phase of Mexico's recovery

began after World War II, with the presidency of Miguel Alemán. Under Alemán's leadership, the government invested heavily in the industrialization of Mexico, establishing partnerships with many international corporations. Alemán believed that wealth had to be created before it could be shared. Mexico had the natural resources to become a prosperous modern nation; it lacked only the organization and the will.

During the 1950s, industry grew rapidly, especially in central Mexico. The nation's cities also underwent rapid growth. It was clear that Mexico's identity as a rural, agricultural nation was changing.

By the 1960s, the country had achieved an economic miracle. With hundreds of new factories, a steady six percent annual growth in the economy, and relative political stability, Mexico had become a model for other developing countries. In 1968, the Olympic Games were held in Mexico City, providing a dramatic symbol of Mexico's growing importance in the international community. The discovery of vast oil and natural gas deposits in 1978 was seen as further proof that the nation had the opportunity to become an independent power in the Western World.

Unfortunately, the development of Mexico's petroleum resources did not solve as many of the nation's problems as had been hoped. The decline in the world demand for oil during the 1980s made it difficult to find a profitable market for the abundant supplies being produced by the Mexican oil industry. World-wide inflation also weakened the Mexican economy, as it did the economies of many other developing countries. Overtaken by such forces, the Mexican *milagro* (miracle) came to a halt.

Despite this set-back, Mexico has made great strides in economic modernization during recent times. Yet the nation has not been able to solve the serious problems of equality and social justice that have troubled it since its earliest years. The present population of nearly 84 million is still divided into a small group of millionaires, a growing middle class determined to protect its privileges, and a huge lower class made up of rural and urban poor. How best to create more social and economic opportunites for more people remains the most important issue of Mexican life today.

Inhabitants of Mexico City wait for a bus during the morning rush hour. Buses and subways in the crowded Mexican capital carry more than a million passengers each day.

MEXICO CITY
LA GRAN CIUDAD

If Mexico City's Plaza of the Three Cultures symbolizes the past of Mexico, the city itself seems to represent its present and future. All the achievements of modern Mexico and all its overwhelming problems can be seen in the crowded streets of the great city, the largest urban center in the world.

In 1985, the population of metropolitan Mexico City passed the 18 million mark, making the Mexican capital larger than Tokyo, until then the world's largest city. The 18.1 million people that live in *la capital* make up almost one-fifth of the total Mexican population of 84 million. If the city's population continues to grow as it has in the past 10 years, it will reach 30 million by the turn of the century.

Mexico City not only has a tremendous population, but it also covers a tremendous amount of territory. Greater Mexico City occupies about 890 square miles of land within the Valley of Mexico, the historic site of the Aztec capital, Tenochtitlán.

Mexico City's main plaza, the Zócalo, occupies the same enormous space as the central square of ancient Tenochtitlán. Some of the stones used to build the great cathedral in the 1500s were taken from the ruins of Aztec temples.

36

The city and its suburbs sprawl in all directions, reaching toward the mountains that surround the valley on all sides.

This gigantic urban complex plays an important role in almost every aspect of Mexican life. Mexico City is the nation's economic center, including over 50 percent of its industry and almost all its leading banks and businesses. The city is also the center of government, where the president of Los Estados Unidos Mexicanos holds office and where the two houses of the Mexican Congress meet.

Mexico's largest and oldest university, with an enrollment of 300,000 students, is located in Mexico City. About 20 daily newspapers are published in *la capital*, and from the city's television studios, news programs, sportscasts, and the popular *telenovelas* (soap operas) are beamed out to many parts of the nation.

In modern Mexico, all roads lead to Mexico City, and children in every village and small town dream of someday visiting the glittering capital of their country. "*Me voy a México,*" young Mexicans say longingly. (The official name of the city is La Ciudad de México, but most Mexicans refer to it simply, and significantly, as México.) The city holds many attractions for visitors of all ages.

This statue dedicated to President Benito Juárez is only one of the beautiful momuments to Mexican heroes that line the main streets of Mexico City.

MEXICO CITY SCENES

Below: **Young women on an excursion to Chapultepec Park line up for a souvenir photograph of their visit. Chapultepec, today one of the world's largest city parks, was also a recreation area in Aztec times. The cypress trees planted by the Aztecs still provide shade for the park's modern visitors.**

Left: **A family enjoys a Sunday** *comida* **on the terrace of the Hotel Majestic, overlooking the Zócalo.**
Below: **A procession moves along neighborhood streets toward the Basilica of the Virgin of Guadalupe, the patron saint of all Mexicans.**

It is not only people from other parts of Mexico who are attracted to the splendor, excitement, and power of the Mexican capital. Tourists from Europe and North America come to enjoy the sights of the city. Business people from all over the world arrive to sell their products to Mexican industrialists and to bargain for Mexican oil and other exports. Government officials from Latin America, Africa, and Asia visit Mexico City to meet with Mexican officials and to discuss problems shared by the developing nations that look to Mexico for leadership.

The Mexican capital is the largest city in the world and one of the most interesting. It is also one of the most troubled. Because Mexico City has grown so large in so short a time, its resources have been outstripped by its population. There is a severe shortage of housing, and more than half the city's inhabitants live in crowded apartments with inadequate plumbing or in wooden shacks with no plumbing at all. Mexico City's Metro is an efficient and modern subway system, but it is inadequate to serve the 1 million riders who fight for

A severe earthquake hit Mexico City in September 1985, bringing death and destruction to the already-troubled capital. Shown here are the ruins of the Hotel Regis, located in the heavily damaged central area of the city.

40

space each morning on their way to work.

One of the city's most severe problems is the pollution that has choked the clear air of the mountain valley with poisonous fumes. Tens of thousands of vehicles, many of them old and in bad repair, crowd the city streets and fill the air with sulfur dioxide. The factories that ring the city spew out clouds of gray smoke that hang over the valley until a summer rain or winter wind clears them away.

Air pollution has become so bad that even the city's beautiful parks and colonial buildings are threatened. The chemicals in the air kill the trees and eat away at the stucco of the old buildings. Of course, people are also victims. One scientist has claimed that breathing the air of Mexico City is like smoking a pack of cigarettes each day.

With all its problems, Mexico City has become an almost unlivable place. Yet millions of people do live there, and some live in comfort, enjoying the same middle-class way of life common in North America and Europe.

In the neighborhoods or *colonias* of del Valle, Roma, Polanco, and Doctores, located west of the city center, the families of bankers, lawyers, factory managers, and successful businessmen make their homes in large, comfortable apartments. They own all the modern appliances and drive late-model American and Japanese cars. They shop in huge malls that include such familiar businesses as Sears and Florsheim. They buy the latest records of British and American pop singers and see the most recent American movies.

Such middle-class people are a minority in Mexico City and in other parts of the country, but they are a very important minority. Their influence in society is large, and their way of life is the envy of their less well-off countrymen. The sons and daughters of these middle-class families are considered the future of the nation, and they have opportunities and choices undreamed of by most young Mexicans. Thirteen-year-old Adrián Casasola of Mexico City is one of these fortunate youngsters.

ADRIAN

Adrián lives with his mother and father in a modern seven-room apartment located in the Colonia del Valle, a middle-class neighborhood of large apartment buildings mixed in with shops and stores. He has his own bedroom, and its walls are decorated with posters of famous American football players.

Adrián is a big football fan, and, thanks to cable television brought in from the United States, he can now watch the Washington Redskins and his favorites, the Dallas Cowboys, on "Monday Night Football." He also enjoys Mexican soccer, and photos of members of his favorite team, America, appear on his walls next to an autographed picture of Dallas running back Tony Dorsett.

The photos of the Mexican soccer players were taken by Adrián's father, who is a professional photographer, as were his father and grandfather before him. During the Mexican Revolution of 1910-1917, Adrián's great-grandfather, Agustín Victor Casasola, took pictures of many of the revolutionary leaders and of the common soldiers and homeless peasants whose lives were forever changed by the terrible conflict. Today the Casasola family owns a store in Mexico City where copies of these famous photographs are sold, as well as others taken by family members over the last 85 years.

Adrián's family hopes that he will also be a photographer, but Adrián is not sure that he wants to take up the family profession. He is very interested in computers and wonders if computer programming might not offer a good future for him. Adrián has his own personal computer—an Atari—and many books on programming. He also has a good collection of video game cartridges, some of which he acquired on his vacation trips to the United States. (He has been to Disneyland twice.)

At age 13, Adrián does not have to make an immediate decision about his future, but his parents want to be sure that he is prepared for a good professional career.

Adrián Casasola with some of his great-grandfather's famous photographs

42

One of the great attractions of Mexico City is the National Museum of Anthropology (above), located in Chapultepec Park. On their Sunday visits to the park, Adrián and his cousins tour the museum, where they stop to admire beautiful works of art such as this stone sculpture from the ancient Maya city of Yaxchilan (opposite).

They are sending him to a private high school in which classes are taught in both Spanish and English. Adrián has to be fluent in English because his parents plan for him to attend college in the United States.

Adrián thinks it would be great to go to college in the States, but that's a long way in the future. Right now, he is busy with his high school classes, his friends, and his many activities. Adrián enjoys his life in La Ciudad de México. He says,

44

and Aztec exhibits in the Museo de Antropologia and the Parque Zoólogico with its miniature railroad and displays of animals from Africa and Asia. The Sunday visit usually concludes with a big family *comida* at Anderson's, a famous restaurant on the tree-lined Paseo de la Reforma.

In addition to his relatives in Guadalajara, Adrián has many uncles, aunts, and cousins who live in Mexico City. Because he is an only child, he enjoys all the family occasions—birthdays and holidays—that bring him together with his city cousins.

The time of Las Posadas is particularly exciting for all the young people in the family. On those nine nights before Christmas when Mexicans go from house to house in remembrance of Mary and Joseph's search for an inn, Adrián joins his cousins in carrying the *nacimiento* (nativity scene) and singing the songs during the nightly processions. On the ninth night, the family usually meets at his grandmother's house, where the children break open the brightly colored clay *piñatas* filled with candies made from his grandmother's secret recipes.

On Christmas Day, Adrián and his cousins receive their presents from Santa Claus, just as in the United States. When Adrián was younger, he got his Christmas gifts on January 6, the Day of the Three Kings, the traditional day of gift-giving in Latin countries.

"We do have smog here, like Los Angeles, where my uncle lives. But I can find anything I want in *la capital*. It is the best place to live in Mexico."

Adrián has spent all of his 13 years in Mexico City, and he knows the capital well. When his relatives visit from Guadalajara, he often takes his cousins on a Sunday excursion to Chapultepec Park, one of the largest city parks in the world. He likes to show them the Maya

45

Santa Claus has become an important part of Christmas for many young Mexicans, especially those who live in Mexico City.

Adrián spends a lot of time with his cousins even when there is no special occasion to celebrate. On Saturdays, he and his mother sometimes meet his aunt and cousins at the huge shopping center called Perisur, located in the fashionable suburb of Los Pedregales.

Like the shopping centers in the United

States, Perisur has department stores, specialty shops, restaurants, and snack bars, all under one roof. On these shopping trips, Adrián likes to browse in Sanborns, checking out the newest computer games. Then, while his mother and aunt are looking at clothes in the elegant Perisur boutiques, he and his cousins usually go for a hamburger and malt at the Ice Cream Shoppe.

Adrián will soon be making another trip to the land of hamburgers, the U. S. He was recently selected to spend two months as an exchange student at a school in Philadelphia. To get ready for his visit, Adrián has been practicing his English, which is already very good. He has also been going over his family's photographs of the Mexican Revolution. He wants to take some prints with him so that when he talks to the American students about Mexican history, he will be able to show them his great-grandfather's wonderful pictures.

Adrián has been taking lessons from the family cook on how to prepare *quesadillas*, folded *tortillas* filled with cheese and cooked on a griddle. When he visits the United States, Adrián wants to show Americans what real Mexican food is like.

Adrián on the Paseo de la Reforma, where his family's store is located. Shops on this busy and elegant boulevard sell everything from historic photographs and fine jewelry to hamburgers.

To go with the *quesadillas*, he will make a sauce of the small green chiles known in Mexico as *chiles bravos* because they are *muy picante*—very spicy. Adrián knows from experience, however, that his American friends will probably be afraid to try the hot sauce. Americans like eating tacos from a fast-food stand, but they can't quite handle real Mexican food. Adrián tells them they don't know what they're missing.

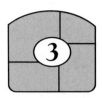

THE SEARCH FOR A BETTER LIFE

Adrián Casasola and his cousins live a life of middle-class comfort in the world's largest city, surrounded by thousands of people who consider themselves lucky if they have enough to eat or a roof to shelter them. Many of these people have come to Mexico City from other parts of the country, searching for jobs and opportunities that they lack at home. They have come to *buscar la vida*—"search for a better life"—in *la capital*.

The main goal that the migrants are seeking is a job—any kind of job that will provide a living for themselves and their families. In the rural areas and the small villages of Mexico, secure jobs are very scarce. Many unskilled people can find work only as day laborers or as farmers

The future is bleak for young Mexicans like these boys watching over grazing animals in a rural area. To find work, they may have to migrate to Mexico's already-overcrowded cities.

on someone else's land.

Every year, more and more young people, many without an adequate education, enter the job market. These young Mexicans want a better life; *"Quiero superarme"* ("I want to improve myself"), they say earnestly. Like their parents, however, they know that finding a job is *muy duro*—very hard—and that they must often leave behind their farms and villages in the search.

Every day, almost 3,000 migrants from other parts of the country arrive in *la capital*, hoping that they will find the better life in its teeming streets. They come from all the states of Mexico, attracted by stories of good-paying jobs in factories or on construction projects. Frequently, the newcomers have relatives from their hometowns who are already living in the city. These earlier migrants help their cousins, nieces, and nephews to look for jobs and to find a place to live.

49

The operator of a portable shoe-shine stand waits for customers on the Paseo de la Reforma. Thousands of people in Mexico City earn a meager living from such low-paying jobs.

The newcomers often end up settling in the same area of the city as their relatives. As a result, many of the migrant "villages" that have sprung up in Mexico City are occupied by people who come from the same country town or village.

Despite the help and support of relatives, most of the migrants have a difficult time in the city. They soon learn that they lack the qualifications for high-paying factory jobs, which are usually held by skilled union members. The only kind of work available to them requires little skill and pays little—shining shoes, selling candy or fruit from pushcarts, mending clothes, or even collecting resaleable items like cardboard and tin cans.

Because the pay is so low, all the members of a family may have to work to survive. Young people have jobs before or after school, if they can afford to go to school at all. Both the father and mother of a family work, and the care of younger children is often left to *la abuela* (the grandmother).

The life of most migrants in Mexico City is hard, but it is often better than the existence that they left behind in the impoverished countryside. The possibility of even a slight improvement brings thousands daily into *la capital* and into other large Mexican cities like Guadalajara and Monterrey. In their search for a better life, however, some migrants make a different journey—they go *al norte* (to the north).

North of Mexico City, north of the mountains and deserts of Chihuahua and Sonora, lies a land of opportunity familiar to all Mexicans—the United States. Thousands of Mexicans go north each year, not, like Adrián, on pleasure trips but in a desperate attempt to better their lives.

Sometimes their journey does not take them across *la frontera*—the Mexican-U.S. border—but to border towns like Ciudad Juárez and Matamoros. Here there are American-owned plants that hire Mexican workers for wages lower than they would have to pay in the United States. These plants, which specialize in the assembly of such products as clothing, electronics components, and toys, provide jobs for some Mexican workers, primarily young women. But there are many others whose search for work leads them to make the dangerous journey across the border into the United States.

The journey is dangerous because most of the more than 4 million Mexicans who cross *la frontera* each year do so illegally. The U.S. immigration laws permits the legal entry of only a small number of immigrants, many fewer than those Mexicans who believe that their last chance for survival lies on the other side of the Rio Grande (known in Mexico as the Rio Bravo del Norte).

The illegal migrants do not come to the United States seeking careers. The most they hope is to find jobs as farm laborers, construction workers, hotel maids, and dishwashers and to be able to send a little money back to their families in Mexico. The majority seek work in the border states of California, Arizona, New Mexico, and Texas, while some travel along a network of friends and relatives to factories in such distant cities as Denver, Kansas City, and Chicago.

Mexicans willing to spend long hours at back-breaking labor in the fields can often find jobs in the United States, doing work that most Americans refuse to do.

Many of the younger people who go *al norte* illegally have fathers and uncles who made the same journey 40 years ago with the approval and assistance of the American government. These men were part of the *bracero* program, which brought Mexican laborers to the United States during the 1940s, 1950s and early 1960s for temporary work in American factories and farm fields.

The *braceros* not only earned good wages (by Mexican standards) but also learned a lot about the United States. When they returned home, they shared their impressions with their families and neighbors. Since an estimated 12 million men took part in the *bracero* program, many young Mexicans grew up hearing their relatives' stories of making money and finding a better life in the United States. Today they head north with the hope that they too will be so lucky.

Today, however, there is no *bracero* program, and the trip to the north is neither easy nor safe. Each year, the United States Immigration and Naturalization Service—known to Mexicans as *la migra* (an abbreviation of *la migración*)—apprehends and sends home nearly a million people attempting to cross into the United States. Many of these poor Mexicans have spent their life savings in making the journey north. Some of their money has gone to pay for the aid of a *coyote*, an expert in border-crossing who uses cunning to smuggle his clients, known as *pollos* (chickens), into the United States.

Even if they succeed in crossing the border, migrants are still faced with enormous problems. At any time, they may be discovered and returned to Mexico by *la migra*. They may be robbed by thieves or taken advantage of by employers who know that illegal aliens are not likely to go to the police for help.

Helicopters patrol the border between Mexico and the United States, searching for illegal immigrants.

People in rural Michoacán waiting for the bus to Mexico City. A better life for some may lay at the end of the journey.

In their search for work, the migrants must deal with the resistance of many Americans who believe that Mexican laborers are taking jobs away from U. S. citizens. (Of course, other Americans point out that the jobs usually held by Mexican migrants are ones that most U. S. citizens reject, such as cutting lettuce under the hot sun or washing cars for the minimum wage.)

Despite all these dangers, the poor of Mexico keep coming *al norte*. They are willing to leave their families and risk arrest because they know that in the United States, they can earn 10 times what they might be able to make at home. Those people who migrate to Mexico City and other large Mexican cities cannot hope to earn so much, but at least they may be able to find some kind of work so that their families can eat.

Two years ago, the Avila family left a small village in the state of Guanajuato, hoping to find a better life in another place. Today, 15-year-old Ramiro Avila López, his parents, and six brothers and sisters live amid the noise and confusion of Mexico City, the same *gran ciudad* that is the home of Adrián Casasola.

RAMIRO

Ramiro and his family live in a much different part of Mexico City from the middle-class neighborhood of Colonia de Valle. Their home is in Colonia Zapata, located on the north side of the city just

off the highway to the pyramids of San Juan de Teotihuacán.

Colonia Zapata is a neighborhood of many small houses that cling to the side of a steep hill. On the lower slopes of the hill, the houses are made of concrete blocks, but the ones higher up are little more than rough shacks.

The Avilas live in this part of the *colonia* in a one-room house with rock walls and a roof of tin sheeting. They have no running water or plumbing, and they get electricity by tapping in (illegally) to a nearby power line.

55

Above: **This poor neighborhood in Mexico City has been given the nickname La Caracol (The Snail) because of its twisting streets.** *Opposite:* **A house in La Caracol proudly bears the family name of its occupants.**

Like many of their neighbors, the Avilas are squatters on land that they do not own. In Mexico, such people are known as *paracaidistas*—parachutists—because they seem to appear from nowhere.

When the Avilas first came to *la capital*, they lived with Señora Avila's sister in a *vecindad* (tenement building) in the neighborhood of Tepito near the city center. The family wanted a place of their own, however, and they decided to build a house in the *paracaidista* settlement in Colonia Zapata. The house is *muy fea* (very ugly), Ramiro admits, but he and his relatives think of it as a temporary shelter. They believe that one day they will be able to buy land in Colonia Zapata from the government and build a real house with a patio and garden.

Like most migrants, the Avilas came to the city looking for work. Ramiro and his father wanted to earn more than the few hundred pesos a day they were paid as farm laborers back in Guanajato. Unlike the Casasolas, however, the Avilas have no family business or any special skills that they can use to earn a living. Señor Avila is proud of his heritage as a *campesino* (a man of the country), but he knows that his hoe and machete are not of much use in a city of 18 million people.

During the two years that the Avilas have been in Mexico City, Señor Avila has gone each spring to the United States to look for work. After crossing into Texas with the help of a *coyote*, he goes wherever he can get a job as a farm laborer. This year, he is in Idaho harvesting potatoes. Each month he sends his family a money order, which is just enough to pay for their basic food and clothing.

While his father is gone, 15-year-old Ramiro is the *papito*, the little father, of the family. Even though his mother is at home and he has a sister two years older than he, Ramiro, as the oldest son, is considered the acting head of the family. He is in charge of his younger brothers and sisters, making sure that they go to school and that they have the books and uniforms they need. Ramiro keeps a sharp eye on their expenses, seeing that not one peso is wasted on unnecessary pencils and erasers.

Both Ramiro and his 13-year-old brother, Rafael, go to school too, but they also have jobs. Rafael attends day school and works afternoons as a clerk in a *tienda miscelanea* (a neighborhood grocery store.)

Ramiro himself works during the day as a cook in a *lonchería*, a tiny restaurant with a carry-out counter and a few tables. His day starts at 7 A.M., when he begins preparing scrambled eggs with *chorizo* sausages for customers on their way to work. By 2 P.M., the *lonchería* is closed, and Ramiro has finished cleaning the grill and wiping the oil-cloth-covered tables. He has earned 700 pesos (about $3) for his hard work, which is below the legal minimum wage of 950 pesos. Ramiro isn't complaining, however. He knows how scarce jobs are in Mexico City and feels lucky to be working at all.

After work, Ramiro attends the Secundaria Nocturna para Trabajadores, the Night School for Young Workers. His classes begin at 5 P.M. and end at 9:30. This year, Ramiro is taking civics, geography, English, and mathematics. Eventually, he would like to study engineering, but he isn't sure he will be able to stay in school much longer. His books, notepads, and bus fare already cost more than the family can really afford.

If Ramiro worked hard and had some luck, he might be able to get a scholarship to the Colegio Militar, the Mexican military academy, where he could learn to be an engineer. But attending the Colegio would mean leaving his family and depriving them of a much-needed source of income. With his father gone so much, Ramiro wonders what would happen if he left as well.

Ramiro's 17-year-old sister, Carmela, left school years ago, after she finished the third grade. Her mother needed her help at home caring for the younger members of the family. Now Carmela has a little daughter of her own and no husband to help support her. She has a job selling juice at a stand in the bus station near Colonia Zapata. Each morning, Carmela gets up at 5:30 to cut up oranges and carrots to go into the juicer. She doesn't like starting work so early, but by 9 A.M., she is finished with her job and on her way home to feed her child and to help her mother with chores.

Señora Avila works at home, doing mending for a dry-cleaning store. She is also kept busy trying to feed her large family. Whenever they can, all the family members come home for the *comida*, the main meal, which is usually eaten around 2 P.M. Señora Avila cooks a large pot of beans on the propane stove and fries chicken wings or bits of pork in a sauce of green tomatoes. The meal is always accompanied by a tall stack of fresh corn *tortillas*, bought from the local *tortillería*.

On special occasions, such as Easter or the feast day of San Isidro, the patron saint of farmers, Señora Avila fixes *mole*. Using the blender that her children gave her for Mother's Day, she grinds several kinds of chiles with chocolate and peanuts to make the dark, rich *mole* sauce, which is eaten with chicken or turkey. *Mole* is a favorite dish of the Avilas, as it is of many Mexicans, poor or rich. When Señor Avila went off to the United States, he took with him a kilo (a little more than two pounds) of *mole* mix so that his stomach wouldn't be homesick.

The Avilas work hard, and special occasions and treats are important to them. Each Sunday is a kind of special day, when the whole family goes on an afternoon outing together. Señora Avila packs sandwiches of goat cheese and *jalapeño* chiles, and everyone takes the bus and Metro to the Alameda, a park located in the city center.

Sunday is also the day that Ramiro gets together with his *cuates* (buddies) to practice karate. His best friend, Alejandro, has a brown belt and acts as the instructor. Because of the popularity of the Bruce Lee movies, karate and the other martial arts have replaced boxing as the favorite sport of young Mexicans like Ramiro and his friends.

Ramiro spends Saturday evenings with his *novia* (girlfriend), María Luz, who is 14 and also lives in Colonia Zapata. Like the Avilas, María Luz and her family come from Guanajuato, and they still observe the traditional customs of their village. María Luz is not allowed to leave the house alone, but on Saturdays, she has her parents' permission to stand in her doorway and talk to Ramiro.

For young people like Ramiro and his friends, Mexico City offers opportunities that do not exist in rural Mexico.

It isn't easy for Ramiro and his *novia* to spend time together, but it would have been even more difficult in their villages back home. Ramiro says, "In my father's *pueblo* in Guanajuato, we knew everybody and everybody knew us. But here I can do things without being watched all the time."

Ramiro knows that there have been other changes in his life since he came to the city. "Now I can earn money for the family and also go to school. Maybe some-day I'll be able to go to the Colegio Militar. At least I'll have a chance. *De veras* (really), things are better for me here."

61

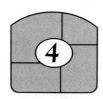

PLAZAS AND PATIOS
LIFE IN PROVINCIAL MEXICO

Mexico City, the home of both Ramiro Avila and Adrián Casasola, has much in common with large cities all over the world. Like New York, London, Cairo, or Tokyo, it is crowded and impersonal, and many of its inhabitants are immigrants, people who have left their old lives behind in moving to the great metropolis.

Although Mexico City is the largest city in Mexico and growing larger every day, the majority of Mexicans still live in other parts of the country. Many make their homes in smaller cities like Morelia, Puebla, and Querétaro, where the pace of change is slower and the traditions and values of an older Mexico still survive.

One of the traditions that still exists

Young people gather on Sunday evening in the plaza of Morelia.

in many of the smaller Mexican cities is the central role of the *plaza principal*, or town square, in the life of the community. Amid the plaza's fountains and flower beds, the people of the city meet each day to conduct public business and to enjoy each other's company.

On a sunny weekday morning, local businessmen stop in the plaza on their way to work and greet each other cordially with a handshake or with the formal embrace of friendship known as the *abrazo*. *Campesinos*, country people from nearby villages, gossip under the shade of a centuries-old cypress tree while they wait for the banks to open. On the other side of the plaza, a group of high school students gather to compare answers to last night's homework assignment.

On Sunday nights, the plaza becomes the setting for a community party. In good

Early morning in the *plaza principal* **of Patzcuaro. This beautiful colonial city, established in the 1500s, has been preserved as a historical monument.**

weather, the police band performs on the bandstand in the center of the plaza, playing stirring John Philip Sousa marches to the delight of the families gathered there. Along the outer sidewalks of the plaza, vendors with pushcarts offer appetizing snacks of popcorn, hotcakes, corn-on-the-cob, and fried bananas, while the balloon seller's brightly colored wares attract the younger children in the crowd.

Sunday night is also the time of the traditional *paseo*, when the young people of the city, dressed in their best clothes, come to promenade around the plaza. The boys walk in a clockwise direction, while the girls move counterclockwise. As the young people pass each other, they flirt and joke under the watchful eyes of their parents and older relatives.

As the focus of public life, the *plaza principal* is the location of the most important buildings in the city. The main government offices are found there, as are the best hotels and restaurants. Since Colonial times, the most important families in provincial towns have had their houses and places of business on or near the plaza. Even today, *la gente de la plaza* (the people of the plaza) are leading citizens in such communities.

Also found on or near the plaza in most provincial cities is the community's largest and most important church. Constructed by Spanish friars during the Colonial period, the beautiful provincial churches symbolize the enduring role of Catholicism in traditional Mexican culture. In the public life of the plaza, *la iglesia* is also the site for one of the grandest of community celebrations, the fiesta.

More so than the Mexicans who live in large cities, the *provincianos* enjoy a year-long cycle of fiestas, each one dedicated to a specific saint. Each fiesta has its own special observances, but all the celebrations include processions, music, and fireworks in the form of a *castillo*, a huge "castle" of rockets, sparklers, and other devices set up between the church and the plaza. At the highpoint of the fiesta, the fireworks are set off while the bands play and the children squeal in delight at the exploding colors.

In many of Mexico's smaller provincial cities, the public life of the plaza continues as it has for centuries, but in the larger cities, changes have begun to take place. Some merchants have moved their businesses from the *plaza principal* to new commercial districts in the suburbs that have grown up around the cities. New hotels and motels are also being built on the outskirts of the communities.

On Sunday nights, the plaza is not quite so crowded now since some families stay home to watch a favorite television show relayed by microwave from Mexico City. Young couples who meet on the plaza may sit on secluded benches and hold hands instead of taking part in the traditional promenade. Despite these changes, the traditions of the *plaza principal* survive in many parts of Mexico, preserving customs from an older way of life.

National holidays like La Dia de la Bandera (Flag Day) are important public events in Mexico's provincial cities. In Morelia, the celebration held on February 24, 1985, included parades, patriotic songs, and speeches by public officials.

Just as the plaza is the symbol and center of public life in a provincial city, the patio is the focus of traditional family life. Unlike most houses in the United States, with their front lawns and backyards, the typical Mexican house is built around a central patio, open to the sky and surrounded by bedrooms, kitchen, and parlor. This kind of inward-looking home reflects both the architectural style of Mexico's Spanish heritage as well as the Mexican family's desire for privacy and protection from the outside world.

Mexicans make a clear distinction between the world of *la calle*, "the street," and the world of *la casa*, "the home." Mexican parents teach their children that they must be polite and respectful to neighbors, teachers, shopkeepers—the people of *la calle*. Above all else, however, children learn that they must love and work for the members of *la casa*. This attitude of loyalty and caring includes not only the immediate family and close relatives but also the children's godparents, who are known as *comadre* and *compadre*, meaning "co-mother" and "co-father."

Within *la casa*, children learn the rules of living that they will be expected to follow

A traditional Mexican house turns a blank face to the street but provides privacy and protection to the family who lives within its thick walls.

A family takes a late afternoon stroll through the plaza of Patzcuaro.

when they are grown. In traditional Mexican homes, the father is the undisputed head of the family whose authority is respected and sometimes feared by his wife and children. The mother is a full-time provider and caretaker, honored for her dedication to her family's well-being.

Boys growing up in such traditional families are taught to be tough and independent, with their education and energies directed toward a career. Girls learn to be demure and dependent; their early training prepares them not for a career but for the duties of marriage and motherhood.

69

Despite the different roles that they are expected to assume, boys and girls in a Mexican family grow up with a close and warm relationship. Brothers and sisters are encouraged to enjoy each other's company and to depend on each other their entire lives. In the patio of the family home, brother and sister play together, and older children learn to take care of younger members of the family.

Today as in the past, a close-knit family is still the strongest social institution in provincial Mexico and in most of Mexican society. There have been some changes, however, in the traditions and forms of family life. Ten years ago, a typical provincial family had six or seven children. Today, more parents are concerned about family planning, and many young couples say they want to have only two or three children.

Ideas about the role of women have also been affected by change. Young women of the provincial middle class are now more independent than they were a generation ago. They often drive the family car to the plaza to meet their friends. Some of them talk about careers in law or medicine, not just about when and whom they will marry.

Other changes are drawing both young women and young men away from their homes and families in the provinces. The best schools in the country are located in the large cities. Young people who want to succeed in modern Mexico must now consider leaving their hometowns to attend college and even high school.

Although some of the traditions of family life have changed, family ties are still very strong in Mexico. Most Mexicans still speak of themselves not as individuals but as members of a family. Even though young people may go away to school, they come home faithfully to spend every holiday, particularly Mother's Day, with their relatives. Mexican girls like Ana Rosa Miranda of Morelia have more independence and more opportunities than their mothers had, but their lives are still centered on the traditional values of family and home.

ANA ROSA

Ana Rosa Miranda is 14, going on 15, and she can hardly wait for the day of her *quince años*—her 15th birthday. In Mexico, this birthday is traditionally one of the most important events in a girl's life, second only to the day that she gets married. When she becomes 15, a girl is no longer considered a child; instead she is a *señorita*, with all the privileges and obligations of a young woman.

Right now, Ana Rosa is thinking more about the privileges of being a *señorita* than about any obligations that her new status may involve. One of the changes will be having her own bedroom, instead of sharing a room with her younger sister Elena.

The traditional *paseo* may no longer take place on provincial plazas, but young people still meet to enjoy each other's company and to escape from the watchful eyes of their families.

Ana Rosa's new room is at the back of her family's colonial-style house, which is located in the old section of Morelia, a city that dates back to colonial times. Like all the rooms in the house, it opens onto the tiled patio, which is filled with potted flowers and herbs. The room is small, but Ana Rosa will be able to decorate it any way she wants. She is planning to have posters of Julio Iglesias and Michael Jackson on the walls and her own small shrine to the Virgin of Guadalupe in one corner.

Ana Rosa is looking forward to some other pleasant changes in her life when she turns 15. She will no longer have to go each day to pick up *tortillas* for the family's meals. The daily trip to the *tortillería* three streets away will become Elena's job. Perhaps the most important privilege that Ana Rosa will enjoy as a *señorita* will be having her parents' permission to meet her *novio* (boyfriend), Rogelio, each Sunday on the plaza for the band concert. And she won't even have to come home until 9 o'clock.

To celebrate the great occasion of Ana Rosa's birthday, there will be a big party, and this afternoon, Ana Rosa and her mother are discussing the details in the parlor of their home. The parlor is located at the front of the house, with its windows, covered by iron grates, opening onto the street. It is a rather formal room where the family keeps photographs of Ana Rosa's grandparents, of her parents' wedding, and of all the children at their first communions and confirmations. It is also where the television set is located, and today Ana Rosa and her mother are keeping an eye on their favorite *tele-novela* as they go over the plans for the party.

Ana Rosa and her family are planning the celebration, but it will actually be given by Ana Rosas's *padrinos*, or godparents. These are not her baptismal godparents but respected family friends who have been requested to sponsor this very special event. Ana Rosa's parents have asked Ing. (Engineer) Rodriquez, Señor Miranda's boss at the turbine factory, and his wife to be *padrinos* for their daughter's *quince años*. Ing. Rodriguez has rented the Lion's Club for the party that he and Señora Rodriguez will give on the night of Ana Rosa's birthday.

Ana Rosa and her mother have already made out the guest list, which includes her friends from school and all her cousins, aunts, and uncles, as well as many close friends of the family.

The Mirandas have lived in the *colonia* of Benito Juárez, located near Morelia's *plaza principal*, for more than 20 years, and they have close ties in the neighborhood. Don Pancho Hernandez and the unmarried Velásquez sisters, distant cousins of the family, are shopkeepers on the plaza who have done business with the Mirandas for many years. They are coming to the party, along with Don Aurelio and his wife, who were the *padrinos* for the *quince años* of Ana Rosa's older sister, Silvia. Also on the list is Doctor López, who has delivered all the Miranda children and has treated the family's aches and pains for as long as Ana Rosa can remember.

Many of Ana Rosa's relatives will be contributing to the success of this special occasion. Her cousin Ramón is the leader of Morelia's hottest rock band, and he has agreed to provide music for the dancing at the party. Her uncle Renald's bakery will supply the huge cake, and her aunts will arrange the flowers at the Iglesia de Santo Domingo, where Ana Rosa, her family, and her godparents will attend a special mass given in her name.

Today, all of Ana Rosa's thoughts are on the party and the preparations for it: Will her long, lace-trimmed dress be ready in time? Will all her friends from school be able to come? Ana Rosa knows, however,

Students at Morelia's Secundaria Federal José María Morelos conduct a lively discussion with the school librarian.

that after the party is over and the dress packed carefully away, she will have begun a different period of her life.

At age 15, her mother was already married, but Ana Rosa has no intention of

getting married for a long time. She is only in her third year of junior high school and plans to finish her education before making any decision about the future.

Ana Rosa attends a government school, the Secundaria Federal José María Morelos, named after the same Mexican hero from whom the city of Morelia got its name.

It is a large school, with 2,000 students who come in two shifts or *turnos*: a morning shift from 7:30 to 1:30, and an afternoon one from 2:30 to 8:30. Ana Rosa attends in the morning, taking classes in mathematics, natural sciences, English, Spanish, civics, and (her favorite) physical education.

75

Like other members of her family, Ana Rosa loves sports and is a good athlete. Last year, her brother Antonio led Morelia's boys basketball team to the Michoacán state championship. Ana Rosa's sport is also basketball, and she is captain of the girl's team at her school. Her teammates have given her the nickname Cangura (Kangaroo) because she is such a good jumper. Ana Rosa doesn't mind the nickname at all; she knows that she can jump higher than the others and hit more baskets too.

When the Summer Olympics were held in Los Angeles in 1984, Ana Rosa saw some of the exciting women's basketball games on television. Ever since, she has dreamed of playing on Mexico's national basketball team and of someday competing in the Olympics.

Ana Rosa knows that it wouldn't be easy to make her dream come true. She would have to work hard to qualify for the basketball team and then go to Mexico City for training. She also knows that her parents would not be pleased by the idea. Her father in particular has old-fashioned views concerning the proper life for a well-brought-up girl, and playing basketball in front of thousands of people would definitely not be considered appropriate.

Ana Rosa herself is not sure that she would want to leave her family and her *novio* for the months, perhaps even years, that training for the team would require. Even the idea of spending two weeks with her uncle in Guadalajara (a *quince años* present from her parents) is making her a little nervous. How would she manage being so far from home for so much longer?

Still, Ana Rosa daydreams about the sharp uniforms of the women's basketball team and about the thrill of playing in the Olympic games. Maybe she could do it. *¿Quien sabe?* Meanwhile, the playoffs for the state basketball championship will be coming up soon, and Cangura and her team have a lot of practicing to do.

INDIAN MEXICO

North Americans often think of Mexico as an Indian country, where most people wear colorful costumes and live in Indian "huts." In reality, only 10 percent of the Mexican population—about 8 million people—speaks an Indian language and follows an Indian way of life.

Before the Spanish Conquest in the 16th century, there were as many as 20 million Indians in Mexico speaking around 60 different languages. After the Conquest, warfare and disease greatly reduced the native population. Most of the remaining Indians, forced to accept the Catholic religion and work for Spanish masters, soon became part of the *mestizo* world that still includes most Mexicans. (Ana Rosa and Ramiro are both *mestizos*—people of mixed Spanish and Indian ancestry—while Adrián is among the small number of Mexicans who have no Indian ancestors.)

An Indian girl from Oaxaca proudly wears the native costume of her people.

The Indians who survived both conquest and disease were, for the most part, those living in either the inhospitable deserts of northern Mexico or in the rugged mountains of the south. Today, many of their descendants still live as Indians in the same regions of the country.

In the great Sonoran desert, the Tarahumara, Yaqui, and Seri tribes grow corn, build adobe-brick homes, and weave textiles much as their ancestors did hundreds of years ago. In the southern states of Oaxaca and Chiapas and on the Yucatán Peninsula, the Zapotec, Mixtec, and Maya Indians also follow the old customs. They grow corn, beans, squash, and chiles in small fields hacked out of the mountainsides, using only hoes and machetes as tools. They pray to the Catholic saints, but they also preserve some of the ancient religious traditions, for instance, a belief in animal spirits who are companions to human souls. These people know that they are part of the modern nation of Mexico, but they think of themselves first as Indians—as Zapotec or Maya.

Most Mexicans today do not live as Indians, but they are proud of their country's Indian heritage. Mexico City's Museum of Anthropology not only displays the ancient art of Mexico's Indians but also the beautiful costumes and crafts of present-day tribes. Many of the monuments that line the city streets were erected in honor of Indian heroes, including Cuauhtémoc, the last Aztec ruler, who was hanged by Cortes. In school, every young Mexican learns about the contributions of a modern Indian hero, President Benito Juárez, a Zapotec from the state of Oaxaca.

Yet despite Mexico's respect for its Indian past, the Indians of today are among the poorest people in the country. One reason for their poverty is that many are farmers who do not own their own land. The Indian land taken at the time of the Spanish Conquest has never been returned to its original owners, although the Mexi-

A Tarascan Indian woman from the state of Michoacán. The Tarascans have lived in this part of Mexico for many centuries. During the time of the Aztecs, they controlled their own region and were never conquered by their powerful neighbors.

Indian masks displayed in Mexico City's Lagunilla Market

can government did restore some land in the form of *ejidos* during the 1930s. Another disadvantage that Indians suffer in Mexico's modern economy is their lack of formal education, which is not a part of their traditional way of life.

Some of the difficulties experienced by Mexico's Indians are undoubtedly due to discrimination. Even though *mestizos* are proud of their nation's ancient Indian heritage, they sometimes treat modern-day Indians as inferiors because they do not understand their customs and beliefs. In some ways, the situation of Indians in Mexico is similar to that of Indians in the United States. The effects of war, disease, poverty, and prejudice have been barriers in preventing both groups from finding a better life in lands dominated by non-Indian majorities.

An Indian woman and her children beg for coins on a sidewalk in Mexico City.

The Mexican government is aware of the problems of its Indian citizens. It has set up a governmental body, the Institutio Nacional de Indigenismo (National Indian Institute), that tries to help Mexico's Indian communities become more prosperous and independent.

The INI has built schools in which Indian teachers offer classes in both Spanish and the native Indian language of the region. The Institute also sponsors classes in modern farming practices so that Indian farmers can learn more productive methods of growing the corn and beans needed by the expanding Indian population. Some INI hospitals in Indian communities provide care that includes both modern medicines and the ancient herbal cures.

Another way in which the government is trying to help Mexican Indians is by promoting their beautiful arts and crafts. It has established regional museums to exhibit Indian work and assists Indian craftspeople in selling their products to tourists and to other government agencies. Today the shops of Mexico City are filled with the weavings, woodcarvings, pottery, and masks made by Indian groups who are learning to turn their traditional skills into money-making businesses.

Despite such programs, many Mexican Indians are still second-class citizens who are not full partners in the progress of the country as a whole. On the streets of Mexico City, Guadalajara, and Morelia, you can still see barefoot Indian women with their children, begging for coins or selling cloth dolls to buy *tortillas*. In the mountains of Oaxaca, some Indian communities are still without an adequate supply of drinking water and schools for their young people. Some of the Maya in the highlands of Chiapas still have to walk for five hours to reach the nearest hospital or clinic. A more secure life for most of these Mexican citizens still lies in the future.

82

MARUCH

Maruch Hernandez Vasquez is a Maya Indian girl who lives in the mountainous state of Chiapas, on Mexico's southern border. There are 400,000 Maya in Chiapas, making it the most "Indian" of Mexico's states. Maruch and her family are Tzotzil Maya, speaking that dialect of the ancient Maya language.

Fourteen-year-old Maruch lives with her parents, her two sisters, and her brother in one of the small villages of Zinacantan, a Maya community located in the cool, pine-covered Chiapas highlands. Like most Mexican Indians, the people of Zinacantan are poor, but the Hernandez family is better off than most of their neighbors. They own a large one-room house cut into a mountainside overlooking a lush valley.

Maruch's father and her uncles built the house five years ago on land owned by the family. They made a frame of oak posts and sticks, which they plastered with mud mixed with pine needles to make thick, water-proof walls. Instead of an old-fashioned thatch roof, which has to be repaired every few years, the Hernandez family was able to afford a roof of clay tiles. Like Ramiro's house in Mexico City, Maruch's home has no indoor plumbing or running water. It does have electricity, which is used for lights and for the family's precious radio.

Like their other Maya neighbors, the Hernandezes are farmers who produce most of their own food. Located next to the house is a granary where the family keeps a year's supply of corn grown on their small field, or *milpa*. On the other side of the house is a coop housing their six chickens and two turkeys. In back is a small orchard where Maruch's father grows apples and peaches and where Maruch and her sister, Pasku, gather wild berries in the dry months of February and March.

The Hernandez family lives in the traditional Maya way, and all the members share in the work of producing and preparing food and of keeping the family supplied with clothing. Maruch's 18-year-old brother, Antun, helps his father in the family *milpa*, which is located in the valley a half day's walk from the house. (Like the other farmers of Zinacantan, Señor Hernandez rents a field in this area, which is flatter and warmer than his mountainside home.)

While their father and brother labor in the fields, Maruch and her sisters work with their mother at home, cleaning, weaving, and cooking. Fixing food in the traditional Maya way takes a lot of time and effort. Each day, Maruch, her mother, and her sisters have to get up at dawn to make the day's supply of *tortillas*. Unlike the Avilas of Mexico City and the Mirandas of Morelia, the Hernandez family still makes their *tortillas* by hand instead of buying them already prepared.

It is Maruch's job to take the dried corn, which has been soaking overnight, to the mill in the village to be ground into dough. While she is gone, her mother builds up the wood fire, and her older sister, Tinik, rubs the clay griddle with a chalky limestone paste to keep the *tortillas* from sticking.

When Maruch returns from the mill, she regrinds the corn dough on her own *mano* and *metate* (grinding stones) because her father believes that hand-ground corn makes better-tasting *tortillas*. Then her mother and Tinik make the dough into small balls, which they pat out into perfectly round *tortillas* and cook on the hot griddle. Each day, the Hernandez women make around eight dozen *tortillas*, which will be eaten with all the family meals, including the packed lunch that Señor Hernandez and his son take with them to the *milpa*.

On this morning in early July, the family has finished its breakfast of *tortillas*, black beans, and boiled turkey eggs before the sun has risen over the tops of the nearby mountains. After the men start out on the long walk to the *milpa*, the Hernandez women wash the tin plates from breakfast and sweep the hard-packed earth of the patio. Then Señora Hernandez and her two oldest daughters get out their looms

Maruch Hernandez weaving on her backstrap loom. The loom is set up in the courtyard of her home, located on a hillside in the highlands of Chiapas.

and prepare them for weaving.

They want to get started early because they are weaving new clothes for the whole family to wear at the important fiesta of San Lorenzo, which begins on August 8, less than a month away. Señor Hernandez and Antun must have new cotton ponchos woven in the distinctive red-and-white pattern of Zinacantan. The women of the family need new blouses, skirts, and belts made in the traditional Maya style of women's clothes.

Like all the Maya girls of Zinacantan, Maruch learned to weave when she was very young.

To make these traditional garments, Señora Hernandez and her daughters use backstrap looms, the same kind that were used by their Maya ancestors. One end of the loom is tied to a post, while the other goes around the hips of the weaver, who kneels in front and controls the tension of the threads with movements of her body.

This morning, as Maruch works at her loom, she smiles to herself, remembering how she learned to weave many years ago. Her mother made her a small loom when she was 6, but Maruch had great difficulty keeping the threads straight, and she thought that she would never learn this important skill of her people.

By the time she was 10, however, she was able to weave belts. At 12, she could make her own skirts and blouses, and now, at 14, she is an accomplished weaver. Even her grandmother, who is one of the best weavers of Zinacantan, says that Maruch will make a good wife because she can weave the fine clothes, blankets, and tablecloths that are the pride of every Zinacanteco household.

Maruch has such a good reputation as a weaver that she even sells some of her belts and shawls. At first she sold them to other Zinacantecos, who admired the fine workmanship. Now, however, she and her sister are selling their work in the nearby city of San Cristóbal.

There is a cooperative store in the city that is run by the Indian weavers themselves. Through the store, Maya women can sell their weavings at a much better price than they could get at the tourist shops located along Guadalupe Street.

Maruch can even have her name on the belts and shawls that she sells in the shop. That makes her very proud.

On her monthly trips to San Cristóbal to take in her weaving and to pick up the money she has earned, Maruch sometimes goes to visit an Indian nurse who works at the government hospital. She met the nurse last winter when she gave Maruch a shot of penicillin for a bad chest cold. (Before her parents brought Maruch to the hospital, they had called her grandfather, Mol Shun, the most respected healer in Zinacantan, who treated the girl with traditional prayers and herbs.)

Maruch enjoys talking to her friend at the hospital, and she listens intently when the Indian nurse tells her what a good nurse's aid she would make. She is very good with her hands and smart, even though she has had only two years of formal education and cannot read or write.

Shoppers in the outdoor market of San Cristóbal. The man in the center of the picture is wearing the red-and-white-striped poncho that is the traditional costume of the men of Zinacantan.

Maruch knows that Indian girls her age work at the hospital, but she also knows that her own parents would disapprove of that kind of life for her. The Maya girls at the hospital wear shoes and bras and have no time for weaving. They live away from their homes and families, in a city filled with people who do not respect Indian customs and beliefs.

Maruch's brother, Antun, has already made plans to leave Zinacantan, and his parents are very upset about it. Antun doesn't want to spend his life as a Maya farmer like his father. He objects to getting up so early in the morning to walk the many miles to the cornfield. What Antun really wants to do is to get a truck like the Chevy pickup that his uncle Jesús bought in March. Then he could go into business for himself, hauling flowers from the highlands to Tuxtla Gutierrez, the capital of Chiapas.

To earn the 200,000 pesos that he needs to buy a second-hand truck, Antun is going to spend the next several months working on a highway construction project. While he is gone, his father will probably have to hire someone to take his place in the *milpa*. Antun is sorry about the trouble he is causing his family, but he is not satisfied to go on living in the old way.

Maruch is not unhappy with her life in Zinacantan. She is a good weaver and proud of her skill, and she loves her family and her home on the hillside.

Sometimes, however, Maruch thinks that it wouldn't be so bad to live in San Cristóbal and work as a nurse's aid. She would never disobey her parents, but she doesn't really understand why they would not want her to try this new way of living. It wouldn't change her—would it?—to wear shoes and store-bought clothes and to live with other Indian girls in a dormitory. She would still be Maruch of Zinacantan no matter where or how she lived.

PAST—PRESENT—FUTURE

Octavio Paz is a distinguished Mexican poet and essayist who has written widely about his country's society and history. In one of his works, Paz says that Mexico is a nation with "a plurality of pasts, all present....Cortes and Moctezuma are still alive in Mexico." In this book, we have examined Mexico's complex history and the three traditions—Indian, Spanish, and modern—that have contributed to it. We have also seen how these traditions have been woven together to form the fabric of contemporary Mexican life.

In the view of Octavio Paz, Mexico's complicated history is a source of some of the problems that exist in modern Mexican society. According to this thoughtful observer, the nation's plurality of pasts is not only alive in the present but also "at war within every Mexican's soul." Battles in that war can be seen taking place in the lives of the young people described in these pages.

As these young Mexicans face the future, they see new opportunities to improve or expand their lives. If Maruch Vasquez decides to leave her home and family and become a nurse's aid in San Cristóbal, she may discover some of the benefits of modern Mexico unknown to the inhabitants of remote Zinacantan. Ramiro Avila might be able to escape from the dreary poverty of the Mexico City slums if he could get a scholarship to the military college. Ana Rosa Miranda could use her skill as a basketball player to find a self-fulfillment that might not exist for her in provincial Morelia. Adrián Casasola's life in Mexico City is already full of opportunities, thanks to his family's economic position, but if Adrián chooses a career in computer science, he will move into an even wider and more varied world.

For all these young people, however, reaching out for a new chance may mean giving up something from the past. If Adrián becomes a computer programmer instead of a photographer, he will no longer share in his family's traditional role as recorders of Mexican history. Both Ramiro and Ana Rosa may be able to strike out on their own and create new lives for themselves, but in the process, they may have to turn their backs on some cherished values of family closeness and caring. If Maruch leaves her family and the little world of Zinacantan, she may not be able to take with her the precious Maya heritage of her ancestors.

These four young Mexicans face difficult choices in planning their lives, but at least they have choices. Many of the nation's young people are not so lucky. The promise of the new Mexico has not touched them, and the future offers small hope of escape from an inheritance of poverty and failure. Trapped in isolated villages or in city slums far worse than Ramiro's Colonia Zapata, these young people have little opportunity to find a better life.

To give such young people hope is one of the goals of Mexican society today. Like its young citizens, Mexico faces difficult decisions as it plans for the future. How to create economic opportunities for more people; how to build a strong modern nation without forsaking the values and traditions of the past: these are the tasks that will face Adrián, Ramiro, Ana Rosa, Maruch, and other young Mexicans as they become adults in the 21st century.

Young musicians in Chapultepec Park. The girl on the right is wearing a poncho from Zinacantan.

NAMES FROM THE PAST

Take a look at a map of Mexico, and you will quickly see the nation's "plurality of pasts" reflected in the names of states and cities, of rivers and roads, of mountains and lakes. The name of the country itself is a legacy of the Aztecs, who were also known as the Mexica (pronounced may-SHEE-kah) in their own Náhuatl language. Many other Náhuatl names have become part of the Mexican landscape. Tenochtitlán, the Place of the Cactus, has given way to Mexico City, but Chapultepec, the Hill of the Grasshopper, has kept its Náhuatl name since the days when Aztec emperors had a summer palace on its heights. The beautiful state of Michoacán is still a Land of Fishermen as it was in ancient times, and yellow mimosa still blooms in Oaxaca, the Place of Mimosa.

Of course, Náhuatl is not a dead language limited only to place names. It is still spoken by some Mexicans, and even English-speaking people use Náhuatl words when they talk about tomatoes, avocadoes, chilies, and chocolate. All these native American foods have Náhuatl names that came into the English language by way of Mexican Spanish.

Mexico's Spanish heritage is very evident in the country's place names. Mexican cities like Guadalajara and Mérida bear the names of well-known cities in Spain, while the northern state of Nuevo Leon (New Leon) is named after the historic Spanish province of Leon. Thousands of towns, rivers, mountains, and lakes are named in honor of the Catholic saints—San José, San Cristóbal, Santa Magdalena—who were introduced to the Mexican world by Spanish friars in the 1500s.

The people of Mexico too have personal names that would be familiar throughout the Spanish-speaking world. In keeping with Spanish tradition, a Mexican usually has two family names, for example, Ramiro Avila Lopez. The first name, which is the one commonly used, is the family name of Ramiro's father; the second is his mother's family name. Mexican Indians often have names in their own languages that they use among family and friends, keeping their Spanish names for public use.

The heroes and events of Mexico's history have also been commemorated in Mexican names. It is not unusual to meet modern Mexican men named after Cuauhtémoc, the heroic last emperor of the Aztecs. (There are few Moctezumas, however.) In every Mexican state, communities bear the names of Morelos, Hidalgo, Juárez, Zapata, Cárdenas, and other leaders who helped to create modern Mexico.

Some of the main streets in Mexico City refer to important events in the nation's history. The famous Paseo de la Reforma, where the Casasola photo shop is located, honors the reforms in government made by Benito Juárez in the 1850s. The street called Cinco de Mayo commemorates an important Mexican victory over the French army that took place on May 5, 1867.

Modern Mexicans have not forgotten their nation's history, and the names that they use every day help to remind them of the legacy of the past.

INDEX